Interesti

Interesting Facts about US Presidents

Weird, Strange and Fun Facts of America's Greatest Presidents That Will Make You Rethink History

Ben L. Orchard

Interesting Facts bout US Presidents

Bluesource And Friends

This book is brought to you by Bluesource And Friends, a happy book publishing company.

Our motto is **"Happiness Within Pages"**

We promise to deliver amazing value to readers with our books. We also appreciate honest book reviews from our readers.

Connect with us on our Facebook page www.facebook.com/bluesourceandfriends and stay tuned to our latest book promotions and free giveaways.

Interesting Facts bout US Presidents

Don't forget to claim your FREE books!

Brain Teasers:

https://tinyurl.com/karenbrainteasers

Harry Potter Trivia:

https://tinyurl.com/wizardworldtrivia

Sherlock Puzzle Book (Volume 2)

https://tinyurl.com/Sherlockpuzzlebook2

Also check out our best seller book

"67 Lateral Thinking Puzzles"

https://tinyurl.com/thinkingandriddles

Interesting Facts bout US Presidents

Table of Contents

Introduction:

Chapter 1: George Washington

Chapter 2: John Adams

Chapter 3: Thomas Jefferson

Chapter 4: James Madison

Chapter 5: James Monroe

Chapter 6: Andrew Jackson

Chapter 7: Abraham Lincoln

Chapter 8: Ulysses S. Grant

Chapter 9: Grover Cleveland

Chapter 10: Theodore Roosevelt

Chapter 11: William Howard Taft

Chapter 12: Woodrow Wilson

Chapter 13: Franklin Delano Roosevelt

Chapter 14: Harry S. Truman

Interesting Facts bout US Presidents

Chapter 15: Dwight D. Eisenhower

Chapter 16: John F. Kennedy

Chapter 17: Lyndon B. Johnson

Chapter 18: Richard Nixon

Chapter 19: Jimmy Carter

Chapter 20: Ronald Reagan

Chapter 21: George H.W. Bush

Chapter 22: Bill Clinton

Chapter 23: Barack Obama

Chapter 24: Donald Trump

Conclusion

Interesting Facts bout US Presidents

Introduction

A strangely prevalent thing about all human cultures, from the prehistoric to the ancient Greeks up to the present, is that we tend to immortalize the mortal. What do I mean by that? We make divinities out of humans, we make gods from kings, we worship our heroes, and Americans are no different. Hercules, Gilgamesh, Aeneas, even Julius Caesar were all "human" figures, and in the case of all but Julius Caesar, probably based on real people and made grander over the course of centuries. If something had cut us off from our Puritan beginnings, and we had no idea what Christianity was as a nation, I have a suspicion that honest-to-god hero cults would have formed around figures like George Washington, Andrew Jackson, and Abraham Lincoln. There's even a painting entitled "The Apotheosis of Washington." that depicts our first president in a classical style, draped in robes surrounded by Roman gods. Apotheosis is Greek for "becoming a god."

Legends and myth circulate about each one, and without concrete recordings on how they lived and

Interesting Facts bout US Presidents

carried themselves, the mind begins to believe in some of the tall tales spun around them.

That's why this book exists, not only for you to quickly and systematically annihilate your family in political trivia games, but also to shed light on some decidedly human figures in our history. To bring them down to the level of us mortals; to show you they were like you or I, if we had more executive power and a professionally-commissioned portrait.

Chapter 1: George Washington

George Washington, our first president, was renowned as a skillful general and tactful politician who secured our country's existence from the British and predicted some of the modern issues facing our political system today.

-There seem to be many myths abound about Big George and his relation to wood. An apt example you be his wooden teeth. It's true that Washington had replacement teeth because of lifelong toothaches, but his teeth were crafted from many different sources; including ivory, human, horse, and cow teeth, and metals like brass, copper, and silver. When he became president, he only had one actual tooth left in his head.

-George Washington was the spark that lead to the French-Indian War by attacking a French fort. The war thought of by some as the "first world war," and called the Seven Years War outside the United States.

Interesting Facts bout US Presidents

-Washington belonged to no political parties and warned that getting involved in such a system would spell disaster for the Republic.

-He was the only president to not have lived in the White House. Instead, he lived in Philadelphia, in the aptly-titled President's House.

-George Washington did not grow recreational marijuana at his residence. Instead, he grew hemp, which was and still is used to make ropes and things of that nature.

-The cherry tree myth is not true and was invented by one of the biographer's to add mystique to Washington's life for readers and to extol the virtue of honesty.

-George Washington carries the highest ranking in the US military that is impossible to ascend to; "General of the Armies of the United States."

-George Washington did not belong to a traditional religious sect; like many of the Founding Fathers, he espoused Deism. Deists believe that God created the universe, but now he's just watching and taking a load off without intervening.

-Before blowing the British out in the Revolutionary War, he was a general for the British and fought for their interests on American soil.

Interesting Facts bout US Presidents

-He was the only president to actually lead his troops into battle.

-George Washington fathered no children and was rumored to have been in love with Sally Fairfax, wife of his buddy George Fairfax. He wrote frequent sultry letters to her and she was a common guest at his home, so you fill in the blanks.

-Evading traditional styles at the time, George Washington didn't wear a wig, and his hair was natural. But he did powder it, which gave it the distinctive chalky white color we know from portraits.

-Old George started his professional life not as a soldier, but as a land surveyor at age 17.

-George Washington ran his own distillery and made several varieties of brandy and whiskey.

Chapter 2: John Adams

Our second president, known lawyer and hater of Democratic-Republicans, champion of justice and accomplished diplomat.

-John Adams was the first president to live in the White House. He spent the first three years of his term in the same presidential home in Philadelphia that Washington lived in, however. The mansion was still under construction, and his wife hung her wet laundry in its drafty halls.

-Unlike many of the founding fathers and early presidents, John Adams owned no slaves.

-John Adams was a lawyer and defended the British soldiers involved in the Boston Massacre. He was a firm believer in justice and later would think of his defense of the soldiers as some of the best services he did for his country. This precedent is observed in modern America's (and many parts of the world) conception of "innocent before proven guilty."

Interesting Facts bout US Presidents

-Despite the fact that he owned no slaves, John Adams was against abolitionism. He espoused a belief that his rival Thomas Jefferson shared; that it was a potentially dangerous philosophy because too rapid a chance could shock the country too hard to recover.

-He was a habitual letter writer to his wife and advisor Abigail, with whom he was deeply infatuated.

-On Thomas Jefferson—he had a political rivalry with the man. They were of opposing parties; Federalist and Democratic-Republicans. Eternally seething about Jefferson, his last words were "Thomas Jefferson survives," and he refused to attend his inauguration. They also died the same day. Some would say they needed each other?

-With that thread spun, John Adams was the first president to adopt a political party. It is different than our system today, but it laid the foundation for our current system.

-John Adams gave the signature that created the United States Marine band, the longest-running band in the United States.

-John Adams felt like he was cleaning up after George Washington after he moved into the President's House, when he found the 18th-century equivalent of red solo cups and beer cans scattered about the place.

Interesting Facts bout US Presidents

-The first official dinner party that he hosted was for Native Americans in 1801.

-Of the first five presidents, he was the only one to not hail from the "Virginia dynasty," as he was a New Englander from Massachusetts. His son, John Quincy Adams, would later become president. The next father-son presidential duo wouldn't come until relatively recently, with George H.W. Bush and his son George W. Bush.

-On a diplomatic trip to France, John Adams gushed on about the hospitality of the French. It was a much ruder, silly time, as these snippets of his diary were sent back to Congress and read aloud, where he was laughed at.

Chapter 3: Thomas Jefferson

Our nation's third president, a Democratic-Republican who led our country through one of our first inter-continental conflicts; the little talked about Second Barbary War of 1815. The man was a firm believer in Enlightenment-era values like republicanism and individual rights, and the president who secured a large chunk of our southern and Midwestern territories with the Louisiana purchase, and who would send Lewis and Clark on their famous expedition.

-Thomas Jefferson was a fan of what he called "the Agrarian ideal," believing that a simple and modest life on a farm was preferable to the hustle and bustle of the city. He believed in austerity and believed farmers were among the greatest Americans.

-He probably had an affair with one of his slaves, Sally Hemings. She was three-quarters European and was the half-sister of Jefferson's beloved dead wife. With him, she (probably) bore six children who passed into American society mostly unknown. DNA

Interesting Facts bout US Presidents

testing has affirmed this claim, verifying a contention that has been controversial since his time in office.

-Jefferson had a very love-hate relationship with dogs. He went to ridiculous lengths to acquire a certain kind of dog he called a "shepherd's" dog, an unknown archaic breed that probably resembled a modern-day sheepdog. He eventually found one, in France. He had puppies by it and began selling them to his friends, enough to where he needed a second dog for more puppies. Then, something happened. Maybe a dog wrote him out of his mother's will or maybe one burned down his house, but he displayed a sudden hatred of all dogs and considered them scourge to the human race, to the point of even having the dogs that belonged to his slaves killed.

-Thomas Jefferson was responsible for expanding American territory in our western frontier, paying Napoleon $15 million in 1803 for 529,911,680 acres of land. He sent explorers Meriwether Lewis and William Clark to chart and explore the new territory in 1804, who returned in 1806 with sketches and maps of the area and a survey of topography, flora, and fauna.

-He was an avid reader and book collector, but not necessarily very savvy with money, as in 1815, he had to sell his collection of nearly 6,500 books to Congress to satisfy his debts. His archive had bits of

Interesting Facts bout US Presidents

everything—science, philosophy, history, literature, and books from abroad.

-Appropriate to his ideals, Thomas Jefferson grew a variety of different vegetables on his plantation, including fifteen different strains of a pea.

-Jefferson loved music and was constantly either humming or singing to himself, and tried picking up the violin. He broke his wrist trying to woo a woman, who never took to him, and his wrist never fully healed.

Chapter 4: James Madison

Yet another founding father, called the "Father of the Constitution" for his role in creating one of the most influential political documents in the world, as well as the Bill of Rights. He was an enthusiastic writer, writing the Federalist Papers that helped get the Constitution accepted as the new law of the land. He was president during the War of 1812, an embarrassing affair, which is what lead to an expansion of the federal government.

-James Madison makes many students look bad, finishing a degree at Princeton in two years.

-One of his most famous acts as president is running from the White House as it was burned by the British in the war of 1812. He fled for his life as his wife stayed behind to secure a portrait of George Washington.

-He satisfies the "shrimpy nerd" stereotype, being of very small stature and sickly with a miniscule presence. He stood five foot four inches tall, and

Interesting Facts bout US Presidents

people often had trouble hearing him during his speeches. He suffered continual instances of what 19th-century historians call "bilious fever" and liken to epilepsy.

-He once ran for a position in Virginia's pre-congress, called the House of Delegates, and lost (most likely) because he refused to bribe the voters with booze, which was a common practice at the time and an easy feat for his opponent, who ran a bar.

-Despite the fact that James Madison was the 19th-century version of a pasty nerd, he managed to outlive both of his vice presidents who died in office. He finished his second term in office without one.

-He was given an offer to extend his life by six days by his doctors, who had some kind of powerful stimulant, possibly gifted to him by the devil. The doctor found some poetry in him dying the same day as his cohorts in politics—James Monroe, John Adams, and Thomas Jefferson, as well as the birthday of our republic, but Madison refused and died on the 28th of June. He was the last signer of the Constitution to perish.

-A believer in capitalism through in through, James Madison suggested paying Portugal to use their navy to fight freebooters instead of building our own.

Interesting Facts bout US Presidents

-Every president has their indulgences—Jefferson loved expensive wine, for instance (who doesn't?) but James Madison was more a fan of ice cream, which, at the time was hard to acquire. He would serve several varieties at his gatherings. Apparently, his wife was found of oyster flavor.

Chapter 5: James Monroe

The man is most famous for being the mind behind the Monroe Doctrine, which kept European powers out of the Americas for the rest of their existence and helped usher in the Era of Good Feelings.

-His preferred title, even during president, was "Colonel Monroe," because of his time in the American revolutionary war. He achieved some degree of fame and was injured during the war by shrapnel in the shoulder. He served under George Washington, with whom he later had a dispute for charging him with incompetence.

-He was the last president from Virginia, ending the Virginia dynasty.

-He was a zealous politician and statesman, holding essentially all public offices. He was a key member of both Jefferson and Madison's cabinet. For Jefferson, he was the minister to France and England, and for Madison, he was both the secretary of state and the secretary of war.

Interesting Facts bout US Presidents

-Monroe was the closest president to hitting George Washington's record of a unanimous vote into office, getting 68% of votes his first term and 81% on his (unopposed) second term. A single elector kept him from matching Washington's feat.

-Monroe was the president under which the White House became the White House. It was during his rule that repairs were initiated from the War of 1812, and the year that he entered office it was actually painted the color it's named for.

-Missouri and Maine became states under Monroe.

-Monroe fell into poverty after his time in office and lived with his daughter until his death.

-He was first in a number of amazingly unrelated categories; the first president to adopt a more modern style and wear long pants, and the first president who used to be a senator.

-Monroe traveled from France to Spain on a diplomatic mission by mule.

-Under his administration, the American Colonization Society was founded and the country of Liberia was born. Their capital still bears his namesake: Monrovia.

Chapter 6: Andrew Jackson

Notorious hater of banks and famous duelist, champion of the common man, a war hero and general who stole an astounding victory from the British during the otherwise disastrous war of 1812. He had a darker side as well; his brutal treatment of the Native Americans led to the disastrous Trail of Tears incident.

-Jackson was a notoriously tough man, and he earned his nickname "Old Hickory" during a march to Nashville during the Creek War.

-Jackson would be victim to the first presidential assassination attempt in US history. A would-be assassin, Richard Lawrence, a house painter, confronted Jackson outside the US Capitol, both of his pistols misfired, and Jackson beat him bloody with his cane. The odds of both pistols misfiring were incredibly small—1 in 125,000.

-Jackson's parents both came from Ireland, but he was orphaned as a young teenager. Despite his brutal reputation toward Native Americans, he adopted two Native American boys.

-He fought in over 100 duels, but only ever killed one man. That man was Charles Dickinson, who insulted Jackson's wife's honor. Jackson himself was shot in the chest, and the bullet ended up a few inches from his heart. He collected himself and thereafter blew him away.

-Andrew Jackson turned on the charm when he met his wife, who was already married at the time. Her husband was abusive and constantly suspicious of her getting around with other men.

-Andrew Jackson was the first president to be affected by a change in major voting rights. Before the election that placed him in the presidential seat, voting was restricted to land-owning white men. A change in policy that was enacted for most states, which allowed white men who owned no land, was crucial in getting him into office.

-Before meeting his wife Rachel, he had something of a wild streak. He was known for heavy drinking, gambling, and visiting brothels.

-He served the role of a courier, carrying messages back and forth, for the Americans during the Revolutionary War. He was imprisoned by the

Interesting Facts bout US Presidents

English for a while and was the only one of his family to survive it.

-Jackson was once gifted a 1,400-pound wheel of cheese that he decided to store in the White House. Before leaving office, he donated it to the public and let them demolish it.

-Jackson is immortalized on the $20 bill, despite never trusting paper money, as he was once run afoul by it.

-He may have been a loan shark in another life. He almost started a war with France over some indebted money. It was a bad enough problem that the English had to play the role of peace mediators for us.

Chapter 7: Abraham Lincoln

Lincoln is commonly ranked among the greatest US presidents, and it's no wonder why. Lincoln was a gifted speaker, lawyer, and statesman, who carried our country successfully through the Civil War and was responsible for emancipating the slaves.

-Abraham Lincoln was also a notoriously skilled wrestler in his younger days. In 12 recorded years of wrestling, we can only find a single defeat. He was also great at trash talking, much like modern wrestlers. "Any of you want to try it, come on and whet your horns!" was a challenge he hurled at the crowd after thoroughly demolishing a man in a match.

-To date, Abraham Lincoln was our tallest president, standing at six feet, four inches tall.

-Despite his lofty achievements, Abraham Lincoln had only about 12 months of formal education. The rest of what he knew was self-taught as he grew up on

Interesting Facts bout US Presidents

what was essentially the frontier; he was an avid reader his entire life.

-Lincoln made his living as a lawyer before being president, but for over a year and a half of his law career, he wasn't certified to practice.

-Abraham Lincoln had something of a rival, Stephen Douglas. They were alike but different; similar in personality but opposite in appearance and politics. A slew of debates happened around the country, for control of the Illinois General Assembly, with Lincoln supporting a larger role for government and Douglas the opposite. They even competed for the hand of the same woman—but she favored Lincoln, and eventually, they were married.

-Lincoln was responsible for making Thanksgiving into the celebration we know today, expanding it from a local holiday for New Englanders to a nationwide celebration. Turkeys still gobble foul things about him to this day.

-Lincoln may be our most inventive president, as he's the only one with a patent. The patent is for easing steamboat movement in shallow water. The idea never gained much traction, but he's still the only one.

-Lincoln was the first president from the Republican Party. Back in the mid-19th century, the Republicans'

Interesting Facts bout US Presidents

main interests were in keeping slavery out of new territories.

-Lincoln never belonged to a church, but frequently attended with his wife and quoted the Bible often. He believed in God, like the deists, but didn't take an organized approach to his faith.

-The play that Lincoln was watching when he was assassinated was a British-written musical comedy called *Our American Cousin*.

-Lincoln was the first US president to be assassinated successfully.

-Lincoln might have been a bluesman today, as he was accomplished harmonica player.

-Lincoln hasn't let death keep him down. Since being interred, his coffin has been moved 17 times and opened 5. Perhaps modern statesman need to consult him on manners of politics?

Chapter 8: Ulysses S. Grant

Grant is mostly known as the general that helped win the US the Civil War, and his two-term his presidency was marked by the great national blunder known as Reconstruction, as well as acts to combat the recently-formed Ku Klux Klan.

-The S in his name doesn't stand for Salvatore, Samuel, or Stanley. It's a meaningless initial that originated from an error—a writo, I guess, as typos weren't a thing yet, by a Congressman who was recommending him for West Point.

-Proving that the president is also subject to rule of law, Grant was once penalized for riding too quickly on his horse and buggy with a speeding ticket.

-Mark Twain, the man himself, lauded Ulysses as an author, claiming his memoirs were some of the best writing around. Grant wrote them to assure that his family was taken care of after he died, as medical problems and financial misfortunate effectively bankrupted him.

Interesting Facts bout US Presidents

-At the time of his election, Grant was the youngest president to serve, being age 46 when he took office, and it was the first political position he ever held.

-Apparently, canaries were supposed to sing at his inauguration, but it was so cold they froze to death before they could even chirp a note.

-During his time in office, Grant tried to annex the Dominican Republic so the US could use it as a navy staging ground.

-Grant was a known human chimney, smoking up to 20 cigars a day for most of his life, which explains how he died—throat cancer.

-He was supposed to be with Lincoln at the playhouse where he assassinated. The regret from his absence would follow him the rest of his life.

-Martial honor was important to him. He stopped President Johnson from charging Confederate General Robert E. Lee with treason, which he believed would have only served to distance the two fractured halves of the country.

Chapter 9: Grover Cleveland

Grover Cleveland was president during a time of sweeping change in the country, and part of a political faction of Democrats known as the "bourbon democrats"—known for their pro-business enactments and high tariffs.

-He is the only president to serve two nonconsecutive terms, one in 1885 and another in 1893. He was also the only democrat during the post-Civil War spree of Republican presidents. He won the popular vote for president three times—for both elections he won, and the one that he didn't win against Benjamin Harrison.

-Grover Cleveland was distantly related to the man who would go on to be the founder of the city of Cleveland, despite not being from the area.

-He married the youngest daughter of his sincere friend, with him being 30 years her senior. It was something of a scandal, originating from the fact that Cleveland was technically also her legal guardian. He would wait until she was 21 to marry. He would die

Interesting Facts bout US Presidents

before her, and she would be the first, first lady to remarry.

-He entered office as a bachelor.

-Like Grant, Grover would suffer from a form of malignant mouth cancer. His operation was successful but secret. To not trouble the American people with his health, he had it done in a clandestine location—his friend's boat.

Chapter 10: Theodore Roosevelt

Theodore Roosevelt is one of the most recognized presidents in American history—with his glasses, big mustache, and bigger personality. In addition to national park reforms and strengthening America's navy, he has the distinction of being America's most manly president.

-On the topic of masculinity, Theodore Roosevelt was chock full of it. He loved martial arts, hunting, ranching, and other athletic pursuits. He called it "the strenuous life."

-On the subject of martial arts, Theodore Roosevelt was a very accomplished boxer in college and continued to practice the sport while being in the White House, and regularly sparred with younger competitors. He lost an eye while president from one such match. He also learned the Japanese art of jiu-

Interesting Facts bout US Presidents

jitsu after getting a demonstration of the ability and achieved a third-degree brown belt in the style.

-Theodore Roosevelt was the first president to win a Nobel Peace Prize.

-He was a sickly child, which explained why he was involved in so many sports—it was an attempt to improve his constitution and make him more vigorous of a person.

-His son fought in World War I, and he demanded a position leading French volunteers into combat that was, unfortunately, denied.

-One of his exploits led to the creation of the teddy bear; Teddy coming from a nickname he despised. Once, on a hunting trip, he refused to shoot a bear tied to a tree his party had arranged for him, thinking it was out of character for the sport. The story got out, and a shopkeeper began selling the stuffed bears with his permission.

-On his way to give a speech, he was shot in the chest. Regardless of the bullet lodged within his sternum, he proceeded to give his speech before seeking medical attention. The bullet had to go through his speech papers, which probably saved his life.

Interesting Facts bout US Presidents

-Roosevelt was a rough rider—literally. He lead a band of volunteers in the Spanish-American War called the Rough Riders who were the only unit to see action in the conflict.

-Roosevelt was also no slacker in the academic department, being possibly one of the most well-read men in history, and reading up to two or three books a day.

-Roosevelt spent some time as a rancher. He went out to the then-Dakota territory to hunt for bison and ended up living out his dream as a western rancher for a while.

-Altogether, Roosevelt and his son hunted and killed a total of 512 animals from around the world. He saw it as a chance to get to know the natural world and its creatures better.

-His family of pets included a lizard, a bear, a pig, guinea pigs, a badger, a blue macaw, a hen, a one-legged rooster, a hyena, an owl, a rabbit, and a pony.

Chapter 11: William Howard Taft

The hand-picked successor to Roosevelt, William Howard Taft's presidency is unremarkable, mostly marked by trying to moderate conflict between progressive and conservative members of the Republican Party and tariffs.

-He was our fattest president, at six feet tall and 350 pounds. He also lost 70 pounds after being president in an attempt to maintain his health.

-In a way, he was responsible for an American political dynasty, just not as svelte and handsome as the Kennedy family. Both his son and grandson became politicians of marked success.

-He was the last president to sport any kind of facial hair—this author is waiting for a new generation of bearded presidents or any sporting powerful mustaches.

Interesting Facts bout US Presidents

-He was something of a narcoleptic when it came to public functions, known for falling asleep for 10 or 15 minutes, waking up, and resuming whatever it is he was doing.

-After his time as president, he once tried to get into a bathtub already filled with water and the resulting wave seeped onto the heads of those on the floor below him.

-Taft was inadvertently founder of the "presidential first pitch" tradition in baseball, being the first president to do it in 1910.

-Taft also converted the White House stables into a garage, as he was the first presidential auto-owner.

-He also served as the Chief Justice of the Supreme Court, which he apparently found more satisfying and fitting a career than being president.

-Taft kept a cow named Pauline at the White House so he had fresh access to milk whenever he wanted.

-In line with his bathing-related misfortunes, the story of being once stuck in a bathtub in the White House and requiring six people to yank him out is untrue, most likely. But he did have a special Taft-sized bathtub installed in the White House before he even took office.

Interesting Facts bout US Presidents

-He was the only president to swear in a new one, and in his case, multiple new ones. He swore in both Herbert Hoover and Calvin Coolidge, not in that order.

Chapter 12: Woodrow Wilson

The president who lead us through World War I and helped negotiate the Treaty of Versailles, as well as one of the visionaries behind the League of Nations, the progenitor organization to the United Nations. He also championed certain rights for workers, such as an 8-hour day and laws forbidding child labor.

-Woodrow Wilson was old enough to experience the Civil War and some of its figures, being born in 1856. Union Troops would march through his Georgia town when he was a very young boy. When he was a teenager, he stood by former Confederate general Robert E. Lee at a procession.

-After the closure of World War 1, Wilson raised money for the Red Cross by herding sheep for wool on the White House lawn.

-Women earned their suffrage under his presidency, with his approval of the 19th amendment.

Interesting Facts bout US Presidents

-As of today, he is the only president who has earned a Ph.D., which he got from Princeton, as well as serving as its president.

-He was a late bloomer when it came to literacy, at 11 years of age. Wilson suffered from dyslexia, which doubtless is the reason behind this.

-He is the only president to be buried in Washington DC.

-Wilson is the man who made Mother's Day a national holiday.

-Wilson suffered cerebral thrombosis during World War I, and his wife kept him in office by forcing the neurologist inspecting him to lie about the severity of his condition. He was unable to even sign his own name, much like the author of this book, who is completely illiterate.

Chapter 13: Franklin Delano Roosevelt

A distant cousin to Theodore Roosevelt, Franklin D. Roosevelt is known for his economic reforms that would reinvigorate the country that was suffering from an economic depression. He led us through World War II, the largest war in the history of the world, and finally, he was a secret sufferer of polio, which was kept quiet to keep his image strong.

-He was the longest-serving president, elected for four terms before dying in office of a cerebral hemorrhage, after serving 12 years in office. His long time in office is what inspired the 22nd Amendment, which forbade presidents from running for more than two terms.

-He was a renowned stamp collector and stamp enthusiast, a habit which he picked up from his mother as a way to release stress. In his time in office, he mandated the release of over 200 new stamps.

Interesting Facts bout US Presidents

-His wife was his distant cousin, and niece to Theodore Roosevelt. As her father was already passed, at their wedding, Theodore Roosevelt walked her down the aisle.

-Apparently, besides Theodore Roosevelt, Franklin Delano claimed to be related to 10 other presidents.

-Roosevelt lived at a time of new technologies; he was the first president to travel by plane, back in an age where flights were far more risky affairs then they are now, and the first to appear on TV.

-Roosevelt had a distinct style of speaking, called the "Mid-Atlantic accent," which was taught instead of learned naturally, to sound more refined.

-Fear not, struggling law students, Franklin D. shared your pain. He dropped out of law school and flunked several courses in his time there, but still managed to become a lawyer, but he never had an amazing aptitude for it.

-He had a half-brother from his father's previous marriage, who was already busy with a family by the time Roosevelt was born.

-Unlike Thomas Jefferson, Franklin D. was a blatant dog lover and took his dog Fala with him everywhere he went, even meeting Winston Churchill. His wife did not approve of her in the White House, but that

Interesting Facts bout US Presidents

did little to sway his presidential will. So great was his affection for his pup that she always slept at the foot of his bed and only let him feed her. His love for his dog was public news, as it was once used as a way to attack him, accusing him of blowing $20 million in taxpayer money when he supposedly accidentally forgot her in remote Alaska.

Chapter 14: Harry S. Truman

The president who took over for Roosevelt after his unexpected death in office, and the president known for finally ending the Second World War, launching the Marshall Plan to rebuild Europe, and initiating the Cold War against the Soviet Union and its child war, the Korean War.

-Harry Truman and Ulysses Grant both have an S as a middle initial, and for both men, it's an entirely meaningless initial, as he had no middle name. The S was there to appease his grandfather.

-He was the subject of an assassination attempt by Puerto Rican radical nationals in 1950.

-He served in World War I, and received accolades for his time as an artilleryman: a World War I victory medal and two Armed Forces Reserve Medals.

-His eyesight was noticeably terrible, and he passed the military's eyesight test by memorizing the letters on the chart.

Interesting Facts bout US Presidents

-FDR mostly kept Truman out of matters of war, relying on his vice president to look after matters of the Senate. He was probably not so much in the dark when he took office that he inquired "War, what war?" but he had to brief on much of the details regarding Europe and Asia, and was given the scoop on the existence of the Manhattan Project.

-He is responsible for ending segregation in the military with his Executive Order 9981.

-Truman started the tradition of the presidential library by following FDR in immortalizing all his presidential documents, sticky notes, and shopping lists.

Interesting Facts bout US Presidents

Chapter 15: Dwight D. Eisenhower

A former 5-star general and Supreme Commander of the military forces of the United States in Europe during World War II, who bested his opponent in both elections in a landslide victory, linked all of America with his highway system, ended the Korean war, and furthered the space race.

-With a title like "5-star general and supreme commander," you'd expect someone like Eisenhower to be a grizzled veteran, but he never saw a day of combat; he was always being shuffled from one logistic or strategic training exercise to the next.

-He waged war on the squirrels who lived in the White House grounds who would often ravish his favorite place to relax—the White House putting green—and eventually forced them out.

Interesting Facts bout US Presidents

-In 1957, he was the first president to ride in a helicopter, and later, in his second term, was fond of using them to travel between Camp David and his farm.

-He added the last two stars to our flag—under his presidency, both Hawaii and Alaska became US states.

-The presidential retreat Camp David took its name from Eisenhower's grandson, who found the original name "Shangri-La" to be a tad too flowery.

-Eisenhower, later in life, grew to enjoy painting, but didn't necessarily have the loftiest view of his own work, saying famously, "They would have thrown this crap away if I wasn't the president." Most of his work were portraits and landscapes, and he detested modern art.

-He continued some of the work that Harry Truman started when it came to Civil Rights, sending federal troops to Little Rock, Arkansas to enforce a Supreme Court ruling favoring desegregation.

-NASA was funded, organized, and founded under Eisenhower.

-Patton and Eisenhower were close colleagues and believed that the future of modern war was not in the infantryman, but in the armored cavalry, the tank.

Interesting Facts bout US Presidents

Their commanding officers did not share this opinion.

-Eisenhower was born David Dwight Eisenhower, but referred to himself as Dwight David—Dwight D.—Eisenhower throughout his career.

Chapter 16: John F. Kennedy

John F. Kennedy was a stark change from his predecessor—he was 26 years the junior of Eisenhower, a charismatic Boston Irish-American Catholic, who handled one of the tensest situations in the 20th century—the Cuban missile crisis—with adept political ability.

-Despite his youth and charm, JFK was plagued his entire life with health problems and frail constitution. He was given his last rites on three separate occasions before becoming president.

-Kennedy was a war hero, and after his ship came under attack in 1943, he led his men in a near 4-mile swim to shore to wait for rescue. While they were waiting, he etched an "SOS" message into a coconut. Upon becoming president, he had the coconut immortalized as a paperweight in his office as a reminder of his time.

-Because of this incident, he received a Purple Heart. He is the only president to have received one.

Interesting Facts bout US Presidents

-The "F" stands for "Fitzgerald."

-There was a brief tradition of presidents wearing top hats at their inauguration, beginning in the late 19th century. JFK was the last one to honor this political fashion tradition.

-Kennedy came from a rich, affluent family, having the second-highest net worth, second to President Donald Trump. He did with his presidential salary the same thing he did with his congressional one: donate it.

-The day before placing an embargo on Cuba, JFK purchased over 1,000 Cuban cigars.

-Kennedy adored animals and worked to turn the White House into his personal petting zoo by adopting horses, parakeets, rabbits, hamsters, cats, and dogs, including a Russian dog, descended from the first dog in space.

-Over the course of his presidency, there were four known attempts on his life.

-Kennedy had some interest in literature. He invited William Faulkner to dine at the White House. Faulkner refused because he didn't feel like taking the trip there. He also had Robert Frost recite poetry at his inauguration, unknowingly beginning a small tradition.

Interesting Facts bout US Presidents

-To get into the Navy despite his poor health, JFK used his family connections, effectively cheating his way into the Navy by presenting a fake bill of good health.

-In manners behind closed doors, JFK is one of the most controversial. The list of his alleged flirts and romances deserves a section all its own—including Marilyn Monroe.

-JFK's wrecked ship was thought lost for some time, until it was discovered six decades after its crash, in 2002, by Robert Ballard. Ballard is the same man behind the discovery of the Titanic.

-Kennedy's own father wrote Kennedy a scathing "recommendation" letter for Harvard where he criticized him for being lazy and careless.

Chapter 17: Lyndon B. Johnson

Johnson was a big man with a famously big ego. A president known for his work for greatly expanding the reach of social security, Medicare, and Medicaid, as well as being essentially the second most important president on the matter of civil rights, and declaring a "war on poverty."

-Johnson had a narrow scrape with death during World War II. The plane that he was set to do a bombing run on, which he avoided by a last-minute journey to empty his bladder, ended up crashing with no survivors.

-His middle name is "Baines."

-LBJ had his start in teaching, which he worked at for four years before moving on to his political ambitions, following in the footsteps of his father who served in the Texas legislature. A friend of his father's would later support LBJ's rise through the political ranks.

Interesting Facts bout US Presidents

-LBJ was known for his unique brand of coercion/convincing that put his massive frame to good use. He would loom over whoever was his target for the day, and get his face inches from his target and calmly tell them what he wanted out of them. If that didn't work, he would use some form of silver-tongued sorcery to flatter, intimidate, extort, and goad what he needed out of them.

-LBJ placed the first African-American on the Supreme Court, Thurgood Marshall, in 1967.

-LBJ had almost no time for leisure; he was a tireless worker, known for putting in 18 to 20 hour days often.

-Johnson apparently often requested whomever he was talking with in the White House to accompany him to the bathroom so that he could both empty his bladder as well as continue business.

-LBJ came from humble beginnings: a home in Texas with no plumbing or electricity. This probably had a lot to do with why he was a bit more ostracized in the Kennedy-era White House and also why he declared a "war on poverty" in 1964.

-Johnson had problems with his heart most of life, with them almost killing him in 1955 when he was still working in the Senate and helping to account for his relatively young death at age 64.

Interesting Facts bout US Presidents

-Johnson was Texan, through and through. One of his favorite foods was what he called a "bowl of red," a very minimalist chili.

Chapter 18: Richard Nixon

He is one of the most controversial presidents in American history, stemming from his allegations of corruption, the Watergate Scandal, and his war on drugs. To this day, his reputation, nickname, Tricky Dick, and blatant public lying—"I am not a crook!" has almost made him a satirical pop culture icon.

-Despite his somewhat grimy reputation, Richard Nixon is responsible for establishing US-Communist China relationships, making trips of goodwill and trade to the country. Technically, Communist China was the unrecognized, illegitimate form of China, as US policy mandated the Republic of China—Taiwan—was the "true" government of China.

-Nixon absolutely despised the media and any role it would have to play in his life or his politics. Apparently, he made his aids write out, 100 times, "The media is my enemy," on a few occasions.

-Nixon raised funds for his first Congressional run by playing poker. He watched the men in his unit win

Interesting Facts bout US Presidents

money, and so requested the tutelage of their best player. His winnings amounted to somewhere near six thousand dollars, not a number to balk at now and certainly not then.

-Richard Nixon met his future wife—Thelma "Pat" Ryan—at an audition for a Whittier Community Players production in 1938.

-Despite not resembling the oatmeal-selling Quaker very much, Nixon was also a Quaker, and grew up in a traditionally Quaker community, by way of his mother. He attended Quaker schools and went to Quaker churches where he played the piano.

-Nixon was very talented musically, being capable of not only the piano, which his mother forced him to play every day, but also the saxophone, violin, accordion, and clarinet. All his training was informal, and he remained musically illiterate despite his talent.

-Nixon loved bowling; he loved it so much that he installed a bowling lane in the White House basement, which is there to this day, if in somewhat outdated condition and in disrepair.

-Nixon was a great believer in the self-determination of Native American tribes, and totally revamped the Federal policy regarding native peoples.

Interesting Facts bout US Presidents

-Nixon claimed he used the TV show "Laugh-In" to get himself elected. Apparently, it worked.

-Nixon was almost an FBI agent, but before he could be brought on, his position was cut to fit the budget.

Chapter 19: Jimmy Carter

Jimmy Carter is known mostly as being a soft-hearted, gentle president, who attempted to calm many of the problems he saw overseas, and at home to limited ability. He faced an energy crisis, and his handling of the 1980 Iran Hostage crisis lead to his successor's assumption of the presidential seat.

-Jimmy Carter came from a family of Georgia peanut farmers, though most of his youthful ambition went to trying to make a career in the military. He eventually ended his career in the Navy early after his father suddenly died so that he could maintain the business, and he used his grassroots ties to help sell himself as a relatable candidate.

-When Carter was inaugurated, he flew a large, peanut-shaped balloon as part of the parade to honor his family's farm.

-Despite being seen by many as a somewhat ineffectual president, Jimmy Carter managed to build a substantial post-presidential life, to a point where many consider it more significant than his time serving as the commander-in-chief.

Interesting Facts bout US Presidents

-Jimmy Carter was the first male in his father's lineage to obtain a high school diploma, and the first president to be born in a hospital.

-Jimmy Carter was a known advocate for human rights around the globe, in particular in Asia and Africa. He founded the Carter Center if you can believe that. He also helped raise awareness of the existence of Habitat for Humanity.

-Jimmy Carter is both the longest living president in history and the oldest living to attend an inauguration.

-Jimmy Carter was good friends with Elvis Presley. Carter and his wife met him before he went on stage in 1973, and they remained in contact until shortly before Presley's death in 1977.

-Jimmy Carter was the only president to have lived in subsidized public housing. His father's inheritance was split among his children and in the forgiveness of debts, so his branch of the family received comparatively little.

-He wasn't necessarily genetically blessed in the peanut trade; in his wife's and his first year of running the family peanut company, they lost money. Eventually, after dedicated research and hard work, they became quite successful.

Interesting Facts bout US Presidents

-An unusual pick; Carter's favorite president is Harry Truman. The reason? Because he never tried to profit off his position—he just did his duty as a commander and chief.

Chapter 20: Ronald Reagan

Ronald Reagan was an actor-turned-politician with massive popular appeal, noted for helping bring an end to the Cold War, as well as expansions in the US military, including "Star Wars," a space defense program. He emphasized personal freedom and brought a new school of economics that he thought might reinvigorate the stagnant US economy.

-Reagan used jelly beans as a way to quit smoking and was famously fond of them his entire life. His favorite flavor was licorice.

-Reagan's wife claimed that he wasn't a picky eater, but he was known to have a particular enmity for two foods: Brussels sprouts and the dreaded tomato.

-Reagan once wrote a letter of condolence to Michael Jackson after Jackson was burned in the filming of a music video. Reagan had a similar mishap in show business, being partially deaf in one ear because of a gun that discharged close to it for a film he was making.

Interesting Facts bout US Presidents

-When Reagan's acting career wasn't going too well, he would pay the bill by performing standup comedy. He showed off his wit after being shot by an assassin just 69 days into his presidency, quipping, "I forgot to duck."

-Reagan played a villain in a movie one time, in his last movie. It was deemed too violent for its original purpose—a made for TV movie, and had to be released in theaters instead.

-At the time of his running, no one considered Reagan a serious candidate because of his status as a non-professional politician, which only seemed to help Reagan's popularity, as it made him seem like less of a blueblood.

-Reagan used a very similar campaign slogan to Donald Trump; "Let's make America great again," identical to Trump's, but with the additional word parked in front.

-Despite his tenure as a famous actor and politician, Reagan was also a talented lifeguard for a span, saving somewhere around 80 people in his time.

-Reagan was the first president to have been through a divorce—he met his first wife, Jane Wyman, and divorced her after meeting actress Nancy Robbins in 1952.

Interesting Facts bout US Presidents

-Reagan's hypothetical space nuclear bomb deterrence plan, the Strategic Defense Initiative, or SDI, was so preposterously advanced for its time that it seemed like something out of science fiction, sometimes being referred to as the "star wars" project. Regardless, upon hearing about it, the Soviets were intimidated, and Reagan's ridiculous, unfeasible idea is suspected as being one of the factors that lead to the downfall of the Soviet Union.

-At the time of his inauguration, he was 73 years old, making him the oldest president elected. He was superseded by Donald Trump.

Chapter 21: George H.W. Bush

George Bush Senior was the last president who had to deal with the remains of the Soviet Union and pushed for making one country out East and West Germany. He was also the president who led us through Operation Desert Storm and signed the North American Free Trade Agreement, though it was not actually put into action until Bill Clinton.

-The "H" and "W" stand for Herbert Walker.

-Bush was the youngest pilot in the navy in 1943, being only 18 years old, and received numerous awards for his service

-He was captain of his Yale baseball team and played in the first two College World Series, and even met Babe Ruth.

-He was known for his vibrant collection of socks, and he seemed to have a pair for every occasion.

Interesting Facts bout US Presidents

Even at his funeral, he had a particular pair—a team of planes woven in to honor his time as a navy pilot. This started when, in his old age, he was confined to a wheelchair, and his ankles were constantly visible, and he figured he may as well take advantage of the extra artistic space with the best medium he could.

-He and his family have a certain amount in common with the Adams family, of presidential fame, not of haunted house fame. With John Adams, H.W. Bush has to be the father of another president, George W. Bush, and with Quincy, Adams H.W. has the similarity of being a vice president in the previous administration before being elected president.

-George H.W. Bush went skydiving on his 75th birthday and continued doing so every five birthdays to his death. On site of his first jump, Mikhail Gorbachev also happened to be in attendance but declined H.W.'s invitation to join.

-H.W. served as acting president for a total of 8 hours during Reagan's term, because Reagan was in the operating room.

-He was a good sport about losing to Bill Clinton and left him an encouraging letter that can be translated into the modern day vernacular as "haters gonna hate, don't sweat too much, I believe in you."

Interesting Facts bout US Presidents

-In addition to baseball in both colleges, H.W. was also captain of the varsity soccer team and played basketball in high school.

Chapter 22: Bill Clinton

One of the most charismatic presidents in recent history, Clinton held office during one of the most prosperous times in American history. He put the North American Free Trade Agreement into action and even had plans for universal healthcare, almost a decade before it became a huge partisan issue with President Barack Obama.

-Bill Clinton was, famously, the subject of a sex scandal with Monica Lewinsky during his time in office. He denied it and was almost impeached for it. His line was "I did not have sex with that woman," which has entered into the hall of immortal American president quotes. Of course, eventually, he admitted that he did, in fact, have sex with that woman.

-His infidelity didn't seem to impact the opinion of the American people very much, as he left office with some of the highest approval ratings in American history, the highest since World War II.

Interesting Facts bout US Presidents

-Bill Clinton is an accomplished saxophone player, displaying his talent on the Arsenio Hall Show in 1992 during his campaign. Perhaps he could have had a jam session with Richard Nixon?

-Bill Clinton is a multiple Grammy Award winner. In 2004 he won it for his work on *Peter and the Wolf*, and the year after that he won it for the reading of his autobiography.

-Clinton made strong attempts to strengthen race relations with African-Americans during his time in office, and in turn, they supported him. A tongue in cheek nickname for Clinton that arose from this was "America's first black president."

-In high school, Clinton played with a jazz outfit, a trio calling themselves "The Three Blind Mice," which is a pretty groovy name.

-Americans seem to have regained some trust in the Democratic Party under Clinton, as he was the first Democrat to be re-elected since FDR.

-His other nicknames included "Slick Willie," which a journalist dubbed him in 1980, and, after playing saxophone on live TV, "the first MTV president" by religious conservatives.

Chapter 23: Barack Obama

For many people, not just Americans, Obama represented a new kind of politician. Doubtless, there was no one who manifested change as well as him to all voters in that historic election. Obama's mission was to try to save the tanking US economy, which was suffering a recession, to make access to Medicare easier for lower-income Americans, and to reduce the number of foreign wars America was involved with, which he hoped would improve our global image.

-Barack Obama is not only the first black president but the first mixed-race president, as his mother was white and his father was from Kenya.

-A high school nickname for Obama was "O'Bomber" because of his basketball skills, and he was known as an enthusiastic basketball player throughout his presidency.

-Obama is known to be a bit of a comic book fan, collecting both Conan the Barbarian and Spiderman comics.

Interesting Facts bout US Presidents

-His praenomen may have predicted his meteoric political rise. In his father's Swahili, it translates to "one who is blessed."

-He was known as having something of an entertainer's streak—dancing on a live broadcast, singing a famous bedroom song by Al Green on another occasion, and cracking a few jokes with the audience on another.

-Obama spent some time in Indonesia, and during this time, he elected to enjoy life akin to many natives. He spoke Indonesian fluently, owned an ape as a pet, ate some exotic proteins, dog, snake, and a grasshopper, and befriended "street urchins."

-He made an attempt at appearing in an all-black pin-up calendar during his tenure at Harvard, but his looks weren't to the taste of the ladies in charge.

-Obama has a few mementos of note: a set of boxing gloves owned and autographed by Mohammed Ali, a Kenyan symbol of life—a carving of a hand clutching an egg, and finally, a Mother Mary and child statuette for good luck.

-During his initial campaign for president, to avoid going insane from the stress of the campaign trail, he forbade the playing of CNN and unwound watching sports.

Interesting Facts bout US Presidents

-As Nixon added his bowling lane and Eisenhower expulsed the squirrels from the green, Obama too left his mark on the White House, adding a basketball court, and invited some NBA players, including LeBron James, Kobe Bryant, and Magic Johnson, to a game.

-Obama is the only president born outside of the continental United States—born and educated in Hawaii.

-His first public speech called for the college he was attending, Occidental College, to actively denounce South Africa's apartheid policy.

-He's admitted he's dabbled in some illicit drugs: marijuana, and cocaine.

-His is also a presidency marked with civil rights—the repeal of the don't-ask-don't-tell policy, allowing transsexuals to serve in the military, and urging the Supreme Court to arrive at a decision allowing same-sex marriage.

Chapter 24: Donald Trump

Trump is something of a conundrum for modern United States politics—he did everything as obnoxiously and boisterously as is possible, and was still elected. The idea was shocking to many Americans, who doubted the former businessman's prospects because of his brash demeanor. For many disenfranchised Americans, he represented something different; an unapologetically nationalist politician unafraid to use strong language and hurt feelings, who would blatantly promote American interests over others.

-Donald Trump is as straight-edge as it gets; he's never smoked tobacco, drank alcohol, or done any drugs. His brother Fred died of alcohol-related causes, which spooked him out of trying anything.

-Donald Trump is worth more than any president, an impressive $3.5 billion.

-Trump has never used an ATM.

Interesting Facts bout US Presidents

-Donald Trump was born Donald Trump, however, the original, German form of his name, is Drumpf.

-Donald Trump has been quite the reality TV star. Besides spreading his bombastic personality on *The Apprentice*, he also appeared in a pro-wrestling feud with bigwig owner of the WWE Vince McMahon. They each had a champion fight for their honor. Donald Trump's won, and, to humiliate McMahon, shaved his head.

-Trump displayed some show business talent in 2005 when he covered the theme song from Green Acres with actress Megan Mullally.

-He has a brand of nearly any commercial product you can think of—steak, water, jewelry, perfume, even his own board game.

-From 1996 to 2015, Trump owned both the Miss Universe and Miss USA pageants.

-He predicted his own presidential run a few times in the 1980s and 90s, and run for president back in 2000.

-Along with having the highest net worth of all presidents thus far, he's also the oldest president.

-Trump has been one of the most controversial and opposed presidents in modern history. There have been numerous anti-Trump rallies, protests, and

Interesting Facts bout US Presidents

marches protesting what many people see as a brash, inappropriate, and insensitive president.

-He is the first president to get in public internet arguments; he's well known for his inflammatory remarks on social media, a trend that started before his presidency, which his presidency hasn't curtailed.

-Like JFK, Donald Trump elects to take none of his salaries, and instead donates it to any of the various federal institutions he thinks need attention.

-Donald Trump got his career start in a real-estate business owned by his father, and quickly expanded into other ventures, such as television, a football team, golf courses, boxing matches, and authoring.

Conclusion

On the contrary to the unintentional cult of personality that surrounds most of our dear leaders, they have all been men, ordinary in many ways, like you or I, but also extremely extraordinary in a hundred other ways. They are all, without a doubt, a collection of incredibly hard-working men—given the stress of their position and the sheer magnitude of their responsibilities—and the aging many presidents show in just eight years can debunk any faux divinity or extraterrestrial origins. But beyond that, they had minds like steel traps, with meticulous, strategic sense and unchecked ambition.

But that does not mean they are not like us; it's not hard to picture Eisenhower discussing tactics on the proper extermination method of a White House lawn pest with a tactical gleam in his eye, or Theodore Roosevelt getting judo tossed for the first time and letting out a bellowing laugh after being put on the ground harder and faster than he'd been in his life. I think it's these parts that are the most interesting and most defining of their personality, as it's what makes them the easiest to relate to for the commoner—the

Interesting Facts bout US Presidents

interaction of their magnificent personality traits that lead them to the "American throne" with the ordinary ins and outs of life.

This combination of humanness and excellence is, despite the desire to make Greco-Roman style art of them, what makes them such intriguing figures even today. A combination of profane and divine, to be dramatic, but it still gives us interesting windows into the lives of men most of us will never know and allows us to see eye to eye.

Interesting Facts bout US Presidents

Connect with us on our Facebook page www.facebook.com/bluesourceandfriends and stay tuned to our latest book promotions and free giveaways.

CPSIA information can be obtained
at www.ICGtesting.com
Printed in the USA
LVHW051227251122
733903LV00005B/442